Change the Wind

Book of Friends 2

Jason Belavidorico

ISBN:-13, 9798622860423

Introduction

To change the wind is to look at the reasons for the things you are doing and where you are going because of them. If either the reasons or the outcomes are not good, when we are at a crossroads in life, we need to find a different approach to our problems. The poetry here is about the philosophies and ideas in my life reflecting my attempts to accomplish this.

Contents

Change the Wind

We all must live this life from beginning to end,

Whether lowly pauper or royalty's eldest son,

Whether luck is with us or against our way,

We must rise and live till our dying day.

Like leaves in the wind, we flutter along,

Passing each moment till the moments gone,

Always seems like choice is taken from our hand,

We're blown away if we dare to make a stand.

No matter what in life is driving you on,

Whether its fear or love or woe be gone,

If it's not taking you somewhere you want to be,

Change the wind or you'll be blown there eventually.

Use the Day

My motto I'll share with you for free,

It is the simple state I long to be,

Carpe Diem it is when said the old way,

But in today's speech; Use the Day.

But what does that mean you questions say,

When you are not the party chick way,

It seems a phrase of patent nonsense,

A rational for sitting on the fence.

But it means don't let a day fade unused,

Don't let this gift of life become worn and abused,

Enjoy each day because won't come again,

Look forward for the next day to rise and begin.

Ladders

I feel I've gone through life on an even plain,

Like I'm doing the same thing over again,

No doors or windows to a different place,

Day in, day out in this rat race.

Looking up I see through the glass floor,

Where people there all have much more,

Selfish they are, not willing to share,

Makes me wonder how to get there.

I need a ladder to climb that height,

A helping hand reach that height,

I promise I won't forget those who help me,

When down through the glass floor it's them I see.

Memory Rocks

The future is a balloon held down by the cord to the past,

Tied to the pain we felt would always last and last,

Memories, like a lead weight keeping us on the ground,

Memories like a carousel going around and around.

But like an anchor, those memories are a place we start not end,

Until we cut that cord, our real journey can never begin,

And as we find our way; the new path winds on,

Saying goodbye; rising towards a new dawning sun.

River of Life

Whirling around in the shell of my fragile spirit,

Riding in the river of life that has us all in on it,

Sometimes placid and easygoing,

Often stormy and nerve wracking.

Riding the wave with all its hidden rocks,

Hoping never to hear death's sad and lonely knocks,

Sometimes taking an eddy to look at where we've been,

To remember fun times and people seen.

Riding the rivers wave is the only game worth playing,

We're all together in this long journey is what I am saying,

Let me help you ride the pain of life with an open heart,

To help you find your way when we are apart.

Cookie

How I love cookies hot and sweet,

Oatmeal and raisin, my favorite treat,

Or chocolate chunks in a brown sugar crunch,

Any or all, I love to munch.

In earlier times a sweet biscuit fare,

Given to men who sailing were,

Now shared with family and friends,

At the party where fun never ends.

So, this my ode to the cookie proud,

Hold it in the air and say it loud,

Cookie oh cookie you are round and whole,

But into my mouth you must go.

True Friend

Hold out your hands and over the miles feel mine,

My heart holds yours like our fingers entwine,

When life builds walls without windows, let me open doors,

When all seems lost let me chart a new course.

You are my beacon on a stormy night,

You are my truth when nothings right,

You save me from myself when I give it away,

If tomorrow never comes, you'll hold me today.

The unicorns are through and i am lost,

You battle to me no matter the cost,

A friend is a friend, but you are something more,

You are the one to live and die for.

Friends Code

I am the person who'll let you be; wrong or right,

I want to be a friend but don't worry I don't bite,

Talk to me if you have something to say,

And guess what you made my day.

Lost in the world of understanding,

Maybe you'll be the friend on which I'm depending,

The one who's good at making it make sense,

Who'll be there for me; stand in my defence.

With me you don't need to fight and win,

For you lose me before you ever begin,

And those words that are sure to follow,

My advice to you; Shut up and swallow.

Hidden Places

When all the world sees are beautiful looks,

Like the artists drawing on the cover of books,

What others are seeing on that painted face,

Is not who I am really in my hidden place.

The words i say when I am speaking my mind,

Are usually eased by my need to be kind,

But the white lies leave me a bad taste,

Except where I am real; in my hidden place.

When I look out at the world of lonely people,

Who look for answers in liquor or church's steeple,

As they go stumble around through life's maze,

I like to invite them inside, to live free in my hidden place.

Hard Rains

Through the storms of emotional turmoil,

That tightness of my heart did coil,

That lightning flash that revealed a road,

 Never showing the dangers to unfold.

Through the darkness, tigers around me,

Will true love for me ever come to be,

Through the darkness i go to my fate,

Praying that love will not be too late.

Lifting my face, the rain to drink,

It caused me pause, made me think,

Will love fulfill me; give my soul new breath,

Or will it drown me; take me to my death.

Romance

Scintillating lights and a dozen drinks,

Kinda Cute is whats I thinks,

Moving young bodies in a jungle beat,

Feel the passion; feel the heat.

Tomorrow you wake to find them gone,

If they remember; twelve roses with stems long,

A night of joy; a night of pain,

Wondering if they will call again.

A phone rings and a timid "hello' in your ear,

Reawakens your joys and eases your fear,

As two hearts learn to beat at the beginning of days,

Love has begun to take them down life's highways.

Loving a Woman

When you hold me with a touch so soft and sweet,

At any place and time we meet,

Though my spirit is strong as steel cast,

The heart within is fragile as blown glass.

See me as wild and strong and oh so free,

Don't try to make me what I am not meant to be,

Understanding me is something you'll never do,

Just believe in my love tender and true.

A woman is a creature from another place,

Devil in her soul with a pretty face,

Jealousy and trust bound up in one,

Tied to you by a knot not to be undone.

Curve Ball

Classy man, Invites me out to a fancy dance,

Moon lit night, gentleman's hope for romance,

Dressed to kill when he came to call,

Sleek black dress ..and cowboy boots; Curve ball.

Another date for some fancy food,

Going where the mood is good,

Going like a lady, dress and all,

Hair dyed flaming red; Curve ball.

Never really sure where you stand,

Will I hold it nice or bite your hand,

And now we're standing in the hall,

Devilish grin, dragging you in; Curve ball.

Teddy Bear

Eyes new to life, the world in his hands,

Loving his mother holding him, giving him furry friends,

Winnie the Pooh and Mr. Teddy Bear,

He remembers them as the world that cares,

Fourteen-year-old girl ready for her first date,

Knew something was wrong when he was late,

Wrapped in tears around that furry toy,

Easing her pain; she waits for the right boy.

Mother and child, with Daddy too,

Filling the nursery like a fuzzy zoo,

From father the bears of early childhood memories,

And the tear-stained friend who saw her love eventually.

Taking the Steps

Holding mama's hand crossing the street,

Away from the stove when getting ready to eat,

For not doing those things causes hurt and pain,

Belief in my mama taught me that again and again.

Young and learning the meaning of things,

School teaching what real life brings,

The teacher knows the lessons of the day,

Trust in them helped me learn the way.

Teen going out on the first date,

Gotta hurry; can't be late,

This is the one, you know it is,

Love was always meant to be like this.

Together with the one forever to be,

Not always eye to eye do you see,

But there is one thing that helps you cope,

The belief, trust and love but especially the hope.

Redemption

I ran with the wild ones in my younger day,

Smashing and stealing I thought would pay,

Till one day I was caught stealing from an old man,

He told me my chance at redemption lay in my hand.

He told me the possibilities that lay before me,

Tales of intrigue and wonder he made me see,

He said abandon this life of hate and crime,

Before death took me ahead of my time.

We passed the day talking of his past life,

Grown children and loosing his loving wife,

But in his tale, I found my dream,

Something better than my life had been.

So back to school and did my best,

With his help I passed life's test,

And when they handed the paper, he was there with me,

Redemption is sweet...it leaves you free.

My No Regret Day

The alarm clock reads early in flashing red,

As I fell out of the covers of my warm bed,

My ride was late, but I don't care,

Cause i know I'm on my way there.

I'm on the way to sun and fun,

Kissing my friend who has some work undone,

I do too but life's too short,

Today is mine to do something more.

So today I'm on a different roller coaster ride,

Screaming my head off as I'm laughing inside,

Knowing maybe tomorrow work will be there again,

But no regrets today, nothing to plan.

Another Day

When i woke this morning, I knew fate's given another chance,

To be with my treasured family and with my friends' dance,

Every day is a treasure to be shared and explored

Every thought flies like an eagle soared.

Let my heart reach out with arms open wide,

Give me hope where the last of it died,

In my darkness, let love show its light,

In my loneliness, friendship make it right.

Another day, another chance, good or bad,

Take that chance to be with friends glad,

Let the spark of joy fill you with a roaring flame,

Let their joy at your life be why you came.

The Rear View Mirror

Life runs forward on the road of time unseen,

Learn to pause and remember where you've been,

Look behind you in the mirror of memories,

Hold in your heart the love of your families.

The road of life has its bumps and turns,

Making mistakes from which one learns,

Like for a gypsy, the road goes on, never ends,

All we know is that death waits around its many bends.

So, what gives us hope, why do we try,

The memories from the past eases us on by,

And keeping us strong is a blast from the past,

Their loving strength all our lives will last.

Coat of many Colors

I am known to my friends for many things,

The hat I wear depends on what the north wind brings,

For some i am the saint, for others not,

And seldom am i the answer they truly sought.

My sister and I have the same colored hair,

But really, we are not a matching pair,

My family calls me the princess in white,

A friend, a bitch, none quite right.

I am me and you are you,

And with my pet, we are two,

So, if this smartass doesn't know your name,

You've only yourself to blame.

Unspent Tears

When they came to me to say my grandmother did die,

I was brave for them and didn't cry,

Now i regret holding the unspent tears,

For I gave into all their fears.

When my true love had to go away,

Never came back for another day,

Still unspent tears were mine,

Though I hurt and I did pine.

Now i look back at all those useless fears,

And I let go of all the unspent tears,

And my heart is lifted made anew,

Happy with you make me to cry too.

Teeter Totter

The sun was shining, and our hearts were young and free,

Together in a playground of the mind we came to be,

Playing together on a teeter totter, the give and take,

Happy sharing our lifes for only happiness' sake.

Then clouds gathered on the horizons of time,

When they broke, heartbreak was mine,

For without you; loneliness was all I had,

A broken teeter totter; a dream gone bad.

So now in my darkness I come to play,

But your sunshine never brightens my day,

But while I live, there is still hope in my soul,

That one day another's joy will make me whole.

Defying the Wind

There are those who hide from the challenges real,

Who to the strong do quickly kneel,

Hide their spirit and passions strong,

Who commit this terrible wrong?

Let that not be you for that is not the way,

Let us meet the world, seize the day,

We fail to cower in a safe dark hole,

Where weakness takes a terrible toll.

Let us stand in the face of the hurricane wind,

Let us face a mighty battle we may not win,

Standing up with a passion both hot and defiant,

To say "I can do it" when all others deny it.

Painting the Storm

With canvas in hand, he raced the climb ahead of the wind,

Coming out of the clouds, he felt the calm in him begin,

Setting canvas to easel and brush to hand,

He started to paint the storm upon the land.

Like the calm he found on reaching this high place,

He found it in his soul and it showed on his face,

Painting the lighting, the wind and the rain,

Eased his spirit and fought back the pain.

His artistry tapped upon that inner peace,

Until the winds and storm had finally ceased,

With a work of marvel, he started back down,

To share his gift to a one-horse town.

Friendship Fire

Around the fire on a warm summer's day,

The wizards and fairies came to talk and play,

Poems to share and stories to tell,

On welcome ears their glad songs fell.

Stories told of ancient kings and fairy queens,

Tales of dragons and places they'd been,

Forgotten lands softly spoken of,

Of mighty eagles and lonesome dove.

Friends gathered to hear the tale,

Of mighty hill and shadowed vale,

And as the night falls and the sparks rise,

Peace and sharing shines in their eyes.

Roses and Change

In the spring, lying in the grass, waiting,

Like me, part of the mystery of creating,

A hard shell protecting from the trials of freedom,

A wonder to be born if we chance some.

Breaking free from the chains of childhood,

Growing from supple green to hardened wood,

Breaking loose in blossom of inspiring red,

From seed to blossom, change has led.

Surrendering the safety of hardened seed,

Give it up for what you are meant to be,

Change is the essence of life and need,

And the rose has shown the way to me.

Roses and Gold

Two red roses were bound today in gold,

Held together in the vows of old,

Living the fantasy world same as real,

For that's showing the true way we feel.

Sharing all that with our rosebuds pink and yellow,

Each one special in a way few can follow,

Letting them grow in the warmth of family,

Teaching them to find the right way eventually.

Life only gets better for us from here on out,

Together we will never be without,

Our little family living to build those memories,

Those of here and our real-life fantasies.

Circles

Circles; what goes around comes around,

Forwards, backwards, no exit found,

How to get off this endless merry go round,

A nightmare forever pursued by hell hound.

Running away from Satan's might,

In his land of darkest night,

Running in fear in total fright,

No relief seen, left or right.

Hoping and praying for all that is good,

Not wanting to be demon's food,

No time to fret; none to brood,

Pray to God; please help the poor dude.

Looking at the Future

I try to write of things unknown,

But often seem to miss the mark,

A move towards friends and peace,

A shot made wildly in the dark.

Where will we be when time is thru,

However, many years from now,

Will the dreams of the past be fulfilled,

Before through Death's door we bow.

Hopes and Dreams

Working all night in a corner place,

Putting my time in the rat race,

Knowing to the future we are going on,

Knowing that our youth is almost gone.

Having hopes and dreams; at least a few,

Praying some might really come true,

Not giving up when times are tough,

Not stopping when the road is rough.

Sharing good times with my friends,

Wanting them to reach the best of ends,

Giving example with strength of purpose,

Not surrendering when giving just cause.

For all this and many other things,

To see what tomorrow brings,

To be the best that you can be,

I am; you are; and what will be, we'll see.

Changes and Chances

When love eludes you all these years,

When all you feel is alone with your fears,

All your plans and dreams lost in the mists of time,

Feel like a call on cat's life number mine.

Love a little, you have nothing to lose,

Even if the reasons are a little confused,

Maybe you'll find a piece of your dream,

Even if it is not the way it used to seem.

For all dreams are changed with times passing,

Where in life everything's constantly changing,

Nothing will ever be the way it was before,

You can't return through a closing door.

Spark Watchers

Starting the hunt in a forest of steam and pipe,

Prey more elusive than the beach front snipe,

Cleverly disguised in a florescent orange vest,

Not very subtle but then ...I digress.

An important job is what they said,

Watch for little lights glowing red,

Keep alert and awake is all we ask,

For you to succeed at this singular task.

So now you're out there in that jungle of steel,

I get paid for this ..is this for real,

And as our group together gathers,

We call ourselves a Campfire of Spark Watchers.

Sister in the Brotherhood

While other girls were dressing their dolls just so,

She was sleeping with a hammer under her pillow,

When friends were working on a style and a tan,

She was beginning the path to be a journeyman.

More than a gender, a statement of skill,

She's climbed the steps up that big long hill,

At the top she meets her brother face to face,

She's here to claim her rightful place.

Her tools aren't pink because she likes the color,

It helps her to be sure she knows where hers are,

For she's not just the girl next door in the neighborhood,

She's also a sister working hard in the brotherhood.

Scaffolders

Built it with aluminum tube and steel rights,

From ground all the way to the lofty heights,

Build it plumb and straight and true,

That is only a part of what you do.

Whether it's all round system or tube and clamp,

Put up In furnace hot or moldy damp,

Hoardings and stairs, hangers and towers,

What do you think when you are using your powers?

While you are hanging out there in God's country,

Do you ever look up and say, " Can we talk freely?"

I don't mind these mid-air chats about last night

But let's be safe; no face to face meets, that alright?

Hand on the Rifle

No silver wings but one of the best,

Trained harder than most of the rest,

Trained in a mission that's no simple trifle,

Trained to soldier; hand on the rifle.

shield to those I've left

When bullets fly, I head that way,

Forward facing to win the day,

The price of peace, I go to war,

That's what a soldier's fighting for.

My family's safe because I went there,

Protected are those for which I care,

I fight this war till peace I find,

A shield to those I've left behind

Distortion

Fragments of sounds, jagged seams,

Discordant sounds, sonic dreams,

Pain growing, hate afire,

War coming on electric wire.

Dreamer dreams, psychic sees,

Future apart, past endlessly,

Plan's awry, broken on time's rock,

Kaleidoscope, each tick of the clock.

Shades of grey on a dark sky,

Past injustice we try to deny,

Guilty past life past innocence,

Tried and convicted; no defence.

Wicked and cruel, all hope lost,

Can't face the truth of life's cost,

Turning bitter and twisted inside,

In the dark of my mind a place to hide.

Dichotomy

I am lost though I see all,

Flying high; fearing to fall,

Pushing forward while holding back,

Bright lights fade to black.

I've come this far on courage alone,

Can't back down; can't go home,

Mind dulled by lasting restlessness,

Going down a road that seems endless.

A loner travelling on his solitary way,

Living through day after lonely day,

In his heart the pain of the truly free,

Knowing this is how it will always be.

Puzzle Pieces

Like a mix of many puzzles' parts,

My life is full of many false starts,

A new phase in my life and family,

Not sure what it means to me.

My clear passage now like in a kaleidoscope,

A distortion I must learn to pass and cope,

Uncertainty grows where secrets are kept,

Failed visions of what goals are not met.

Clearer vision needed for my present way,

Take me from the darkness into the day,

Fit my truth into the greater whole,

Help me finish the puzzle of life and my soul.

Pageant of Changes

Holding the cloak tighter she let the roan mare take her away,

She wonders what she has started on this very day,

Before this he was nothing to her,

And now he is all that to her is dear.

The cold wind blowing feels like the fear in her heart,

How to tell the family of which she is a part,

That one of her hated enemy is her dream,

And that she needs him, for all that means.

The horse shied, sensing her restless mood,

Perhaps he felt the risk she took too,

And though she knew the difficulty her life would take,

Still she would keep the promises that on this day were made.

Apartheid Denied

Let the pain of my people not be forgotten,

Grown in a land of rules misbegotten,

Under the cruel mastery of apartheid,

A land where my freedom was long denied.

Facing the spotlight of the world's righteous wrath,

Those responsible were forced to change their path,

Returned my freedom to be a real person,

Giving me credit for all that I've done.

Let there be punishment for those who deserve,

But let there be peace with who helped me preserve,

The strength of my soul and not a spirit full of hate,

Their friendship and love made it worth the wait.

For Tulu.. Actress of the play

Fashion's Mirror

Strut my stuff for your critique,

Spin around, show my physique,

What I wear is where you have your true focus,

The maker of my clothes the reason for your fuss.

Wearing these wild and wonderful things,

I get to see what the future brings,

Yet you can't seem to see me here,

To you I am only fashion's mirror.

My fears I'll keep deep inside,

Cold I'll look for who are outside,

Friends I'll have but fear to embrace,

Afraid they'll see the loneliness of my fate.

Blissful Shopper

The lovers of my life can't compare to this,

The joy of shoes and my shopping bliss,

If there is one thing my lovers lack,

When they fail to please; can't send them back.

Taken anew by another new shade,

When the lustre of this one fades,

Lovers however don't seem to go away,

Always there begging for a chance to stay.

At my place I check the display,

Velvet shades amid my sensual day,

If lovers gave me highs like this shopping spree,

Then out of bed, I'd don't think I'll ever be.

Birds and Butterflies

Birds and butterflies fly through our lives,

 But not as high as my love and I,

Together we have reached the moon and stars,

As so in love together is where we are.

Little acts of kindness add up to such bliss,

For all you have done, here is mine, a kiss,

Sharing our work and a whole lot of joy,

Sharing our life, one girl and one boy.

So, after a day at the ice cream shop,

To the Blue Moon for barley and hops,

The glow of the fire reflects the glow in your eyes,

The love in our hearts, a glow that never dies.

My Heart

My heart is mine and mine alone,

Still of flesh; not made of stone,

True to myself, need not change for you,

Take me as I am; don't look for something new.

There is no mirror clearer than what I see,

Don't think you'll be the one to change me,

For my path is chosen by my own compass,

And to that one course I'll keep fast.

The changes you demand will never come,

Nothing to do as the deed is done,

I am me and nothing more,

Not enough; there's the door.

In A Cozy Chair

Sitting in a cozy chair by the fire, sipping cider,

Living memories of a mighty empire,

Travelled the world in ships so fine,

Adding to our world shoreline by shoreline.

At our height, culture was our gift freely given to all,

Tales from Shakespeare were ours to tell,

Giving our strength to bring peace to the land,

Taking our children and leading them hand in hand.

But children grow to be men and women,

They look for their own dreams then,

As we look at where our dream has gone,

We take pleasure in the seeds we have sown.

For Us

So long and forever it seems we've been apart,

So far, I've travelled without being heart to heart,

With the one I love, I need and cherish,

To return to your arms my deepest wish.

Maybe I can't make these words come out right,

But then again maybe this time there's a way I might,

Give you the love I feel for you,

And let you know it's so honest and true.

When the friends have been and gone,

The lights are off and I'm alone,

The tears I cry for how I want it to be,

Where the light fades to just you and me.

The Path is Long

When the fires of hell seem close and warm,

Remember there is never a rainbow without first cloud and storm,

And even when the love of your life has lost their way,

Never give up on one you can't stop thinking about every day.

The path through life is a long and hidden one,

Passing through its fog is how you get it done,

No day starts without the darker night,

The wrong one comes before you meet the right.

When you find the one who touches your soul,

And the love they give makes you whole,

Remember they are human and make mistakes too,

Think of them well; they have off days like you.

Life to Life

Growing up, you raised me to love and care

Now its my turn, the gift of life to share,

Your need was great but not so much,

For one I love and live to touch.

Take this gift a part of me,

Know it's given freely,

Let it make you well and through the years,

I'll see your thanks with your loving tears.

Surprise

Walking down the street with my shoulders bent,

Feeling down, too much wrong in the day's events,

Cloudy skies and it starts to rain,

Thinking tomorrow will be the same thing again.

Opening the door feeling morose and blue,

Looking forward to the time with you,

Suddenly friends jump out, flashing lights in my eyes,

A drink in my hand, your kiss on my lips; "Hey baby Surprize".

Its the birthday I completely forgot,

Been here a few years, not really a lot,

With friends here, I stop feeling so sad,

Even tomorrow won't be all that bad.

Bitter Cup

Fill your glass with love and drink it up,

Discover the bitterness of a loving cup,

When it is shared by one not two,

It takes on a darker hue.

In this dark night of my soul, I am alone,

You aren't there, can't get you on the phone,

Leaving that cup, I go out into the night,

Light mist that feels so right.

Washed clean by natures shower,

I regain my living power,

Your leaving is a beginning not an end,

As day brings night's end.

My Insomnia

Living my life out of a bad movie script,

That's what happens when you are an insomniac,

The winds howl right through your sleep,

Messing with the hours you are trying to keep.

Wishing the role of Wonder Woman,

Winning the battle with the sandman,

Taking from him an extra dose,

So you can sleep forever, head to toes.

Instead you're playing Sleepless in Bed,

Nowhere as good as the movie said,

Counting the sheep, crickets, maybe the bumble bee,

Giving up; lets watch the late-night movie.

In the Shadows

In the shadows of far away,

In the dreams of yesterday,

Where the heart of love does truly lie,

Where hopes live and fears die.

Where the path was clear now shrouded in mist,

The frost of pain the living trees has kissed,

Silence holds us in its untender grasp,

Till knowledge can free us at last.

Depression or anger is what drives us now,

To move forward or backwards we know not how,

The truth of us a painful secret,

One that I never wish to forget.

Gentle Touch

On that day in an explosion of pain,

The world changed; never to be the same,

When your frustration seems to be too much,

Remember those around you with a gentle touch.

The hurt can cut you to your very soul,

Never to be gone; never to be whole,

But when the loving friends come to be with you,

Remember they are also are hurting too.

Someone they love has lost a piece of who they were,

They are troubled to see it in someone so dear,

Reach out them and hide your fears,

Know they love you and share your tears.

A gentle touch is the way you touch their hearts,

Don't hold too tight; it will break them apart,

Hear the words they cannot say,

Feel the love for you, here today.

Ocean mist

Standing on the edge of a mysterious sea,

Crashing waves throw mist before me,

In this place with strangers and friends,

Where rock begins and mellow ends.

Standing in the spray of ocean mist,

With a cool drink kissing my lips,

And Neptune's embrace clouding my mind,

No haunting memories troubling from behind.

Here in this club I'm safe by the sea,

No future plans; just living to be,

Protected by the ocean and lost in the sound,

I'm finally safe; on solid ground.

Silver Lining

Every storm cloud must have a silver lining,

Even Snow White waits for her Prince Charming,

And though it was hard to smile all the while,

She held her heart to walk that final mile.

Love is a word found in rhyme and doodles,

Given to cats and dogs, even yappy poodles,

Bound to our hearts in meaning clear,

Given by our souls to someone dear.

So, when life sends you a frown,

And pain and fear get you down,

Give yourself a slap and open your eyes,

Laugh a little; brings the world down to your size.

Balance

The sun rises in glorious tribulation to the days beginning,

And fades away to begin the quiet evening,

Night passes to noon day sun,

Balance is kept, the world turns on.

Forest grows in mighty splendor,

Till its felled by furious fire,

Destruction must balance creations view,

To let creation rebuild anew.

So let me paint a picture in rhyme,

Of what some call the wheel of time,

Circle of Life that natives sang,

And others called Yin and Yang.

This is the balance of existence,

Filled with life's evidence,

But all must pass through death's dark doorway,

To let the young have their day.

Castle Rock

In the heart of the sunset land,

Riding my bike along golden sands,

My spirit calmed by oceans quiet face,

Breathing its scent and salty taste.

Feeling the power of your travelling need,

Taking you where your dreams will lead,

To Castle Rock; a club by the seas,

To join your friends like a band of gypsies.

At the end of the night when all is fine,

Your head is spinning from mighty fine wine,

The taxi takes you to the rising sun,

To rest your head as a new day is begun.

Mystic Pool

As the night settles on the lonely earth,

I walk the quiet places where peace takes birth,

And I find myself at the edge of a pool so still,

Like a sheet of glass above a window sill.

Leaving my clothes on a friendly tree,

I enter the water, moving gently,

Cold so sharp, it takes my breath away,

In that pool looking so dark and fey.

As the cold swallows me whole,

I feel the chill smooth my soul,

And in that moment of destiny,

I feel my spirit finally free.

Japanese Dream

May apple blossoms fall on the waters of your soul,

And ease your life's burdensome toll,

Let your ears be filled with music so serene,

Your eyes opened to beauty never seen.

Hints of saffron blow on the breeze,

Hints of cinnamon waft from exotic trees,

In this land of Oriental nights,

Lit by paper mache candle lights.

Take Me as I Am

Here I stand with all my nuts and bolts exposed,

And to answer the questions you posed,

I am rough around the edges right now,

But take this unfinished me and let me grow.

Don't play games with this heart of mine,

For it has been fooled at another time,

Too many times talking and taking chances,

Ending up hurting at the last dances.

Broken promises and promises made,

Are much of my life to date,

So take me as I am, this rough mold,

Take me for I'm yours to hold.

Man Alone

When the dawn was breaking, I saw my love for you,

At the heart of me was a light shiny and new,

Blinded by the light I couldn't see,

That the time wasn't quite right for you and me.

I was there for you as a lover and friend,

And I will love you now until the end,

But the truth you needed was not mine to give,

I hope you can find it in you to forgive.

Where once we found a way to talk,

Now we close our eyes and walk,

Your truth and mine have grown apart,

Now I am alone with a broken heart.

The walls between us are only time and space,

How I long to again see your face,

What we had might be gone for good,

Where we go now depends on your mood.

Let these words speak of my pain,

Let not the angry words be spoken again,

Let the old dream die and begin the new,

Let the dream be born of me and you.

Good Bye

In the tangled web of life and need,

On my very heart's blood, you did feed,

Till a pale imitation of myself there was,

And your coldness was the cause.

Never got the chance to say my pain,

Never got to say never want you again,

All the need and now all the hurt,

Never be here; always apart.

All the dragons of my heart roar,

As I push you out of my life's door,

The friends who really matter are still here,

Helping burn your memory to char and sere.

Two Apart

In the shadows of far away,

In the dreams of yesterday,

Where the heart of love does truly lie,

Where hopes live and fears die.

Where the path was clear now shrouded in mist,

The frost of pain has the living tree kissed,

Silence holds us in its untender grasp,

Till tru knowledge frees us at last.

Depression or anger is what drives us now,

To move forward or backward we know not how,

The truth of us a painful secret,

Yet it's one I won't forget.

Mystic Touch

Wizards hear the truth in dreams,

Where life and death are not what they seem,

Where mirrors tell lies and mud isn't thicker than water,

Where my love is strong for the one that matters.

Hold me close when the magic is strong,

Let the power surge through like a song,

Feel my touch; burns like fire,

Taste my kiss; make me higher.

Look to the sky on a mystic night,

While sitting there by the firelight,

As I look at where you are,

See me; I'm a Star.

Star of my Last Day

Through life the world we are on goes around,

All of us here don't know where we're bound,

Up ahead of us is a clouded way,

No telling when it's our last day.

Never put off telling the loved ones how you care,

For you never know when they won't be there,

Hold the hand of someone you find wrong,

For tomorrow you may sing death's sad song.

Dance when the music can't be heard,

Sing of challenges that you have dared,

For if it's you for whom the path ends,

Your joy is the memory for loving friends.

Cancer; the Hope

Deep inside my dear friends' body,

A piece of genetics turns shoddy,

And a part of them becomes a mortal danger,

The beginning of a disease called cancer.

Known under many names over the years,

Subject of many of our darkest fears,

Takes our loved ones and eats their spirit away,

Until they leave us on a dark and gloomy day.

Yet in this time exists a glimmer of hope,

New ways to help; new ways to help cope,

Its a start until we beat the disease,

Take it out; knock it to its knees.

Everyday Heroes

Never fired a shot or fought in a war,

Never a burning building or a sinking car,

But facing difficult choices makes them heroes none the less,

Their courage takes them above the rest; puts them up with the best.

My hero was challenged to give up hair for a while,

To raise money and to give sick children a smile,

A challenge she accepted, with a qualm or two,

But still a task she felt more than capable to do.

Now those children can smile more because of her sacrifice,

For her it's Sinead O'Connor with a hint of spice,

And though I may not see her today or tomorrow,

I'll always think of her as my everyday hero.

Dusty Rooms

Memories of gifts God has taken away,

Bittersweet thoughts of only a moment or a day,

Shared with those around us,

Hollow rooms filled with dust.

Dreams broken are seldom wholly healed again,

Try as we may we can't forget what happened,

Holding tight to treasures of the mind,

Looking for peace; looking for a sign.

But after the darkest night comes a brighter morn,

hearts can be mended though broken and torn,

Life goes on to other and different dreams

Eases the pain of yesterday and what might have been.

Empty Chairs

Places at the table empty and bare,

Missing the people who should be there,

They are gone from me for many a year,

I'll get by after I cry the tears.

Places at my table for my family dear,

Though I know they will never be here,

Setting a place, reflecting a dream of mine,

For memories lost in the mists of time.

I haven't really set a table except in my mind,

Haven't set out the flowers and silver, plates and wine,

A pleasant dream of us is all this can ever be,

A loving way of remembering the time of us three.

Pillars of My World

My balance is gone, the world off kilter,

Somethings missing in loves golden filter,

Feeling lost in a battle with Death's banner unfurled,

An empty place where once stood the pillars of my world.

I miss your words of gentle guidance,

The approval you showed in every glance,

You were the anchor of my kite in life's wind,

Now your passing leaves me at wits end.

Waking from a dream of holding your hand,

Trying to stop the flow of tears though I can't,

Memories of you are all I have left,

Loving and losing you; I am bereft.

Olive

Born of England in Staffordshire,

Lived through war, times so dire,

Till a man came and he took her hand,

Brought her as a war bride to this land.

Loved that man till the day he died,

Raised two children to be dignified,

Met a new man steadfast and true,

And found she could love him too.

Now she has come to the end of life,

Been a loving mother and devoted wife,

She lived a life that was full and free,

Now has gone to dwell in God's eternity.

Nicholas

One of our family has passed from mortal ken,

Leaving behind his family and friends,

And if he were here with us today,

I believe this is what to us he would say,

I left behind the living coil,

Ended my time of pain and toil,

Remember me when I was healthy and strong,

Before those times when things went wrong.

Drink to me and do drink deep,

Do not be sad and do not weep,

For I reach back to you from a better place,

Remember me well with a smile on your face.

Remember Her Well

My best friend passed on this New Years Day,

Her life ended and she went away,

Her leaving us no one could foretell,

But I ask you please; Remember her well.

Remember her happiness in better times,

Forget the sadness; life's bitter wines,

Keep her memory after life's final bell.

Always and forever; Remember her well.

My mother, my guide my lifelong friend,

With you more minutes I wish I could spend,

The dreams we could share and stories to tell,

So, join with me as we Remember her well.

www.ingramcontent.com/pod-product-compliance
Lightning Source LLC
Chambersburg PA
CBHW020500160726
47991CB00007B/2738